S&D TEXTILES

THE FAMOUS FABRIC SHOP

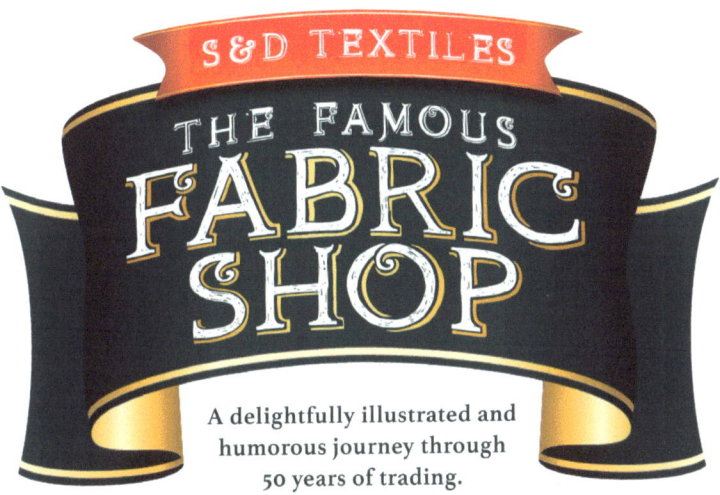

A delightfully illustrated and
humorous journey through
50 years of trading.

Copyright © 2023 by Kensington Gardens Brighton

Cover design by Spiffing Covers Ltd

All rights reserved

Published by Firsht & Foremost Publishing
Paperback ISBN: 978-1-7384822-0-7

No part of this book may be reproduced in any form or by any electronic or mechanical means including information storage and retrieval systems, without permission in writing from the author. The only exception is by a reviewer, who may quote short excerpts in a review.

This book is a work of fiction. Names, characters, places, and incidents either are products of the author's imagination or are used fictitiously. Any resemblance to actual persons, living or dead, events, or locales is entirely coincidental.

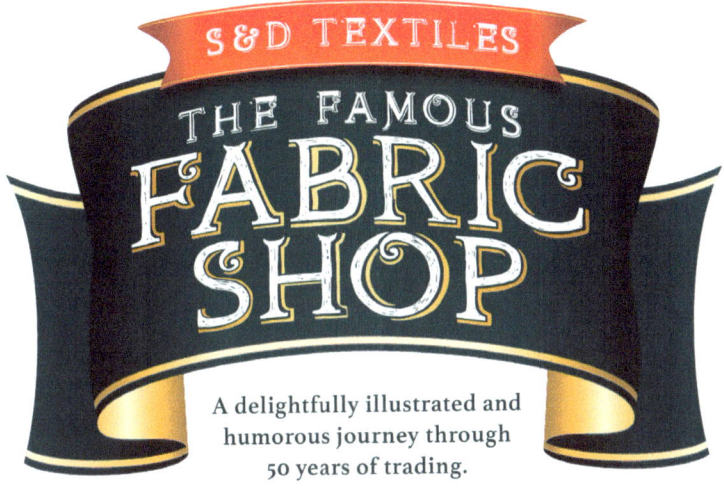

A delightfully illustrated and humorous journey through 50 years of trading.

1960-2007

Genuine and funny questions from customers of 50 years trading in S&D Textiles, the Aladdin's cave fabric shop and forecourt, located in Kensington Gardens, Brighton, East Sussex.

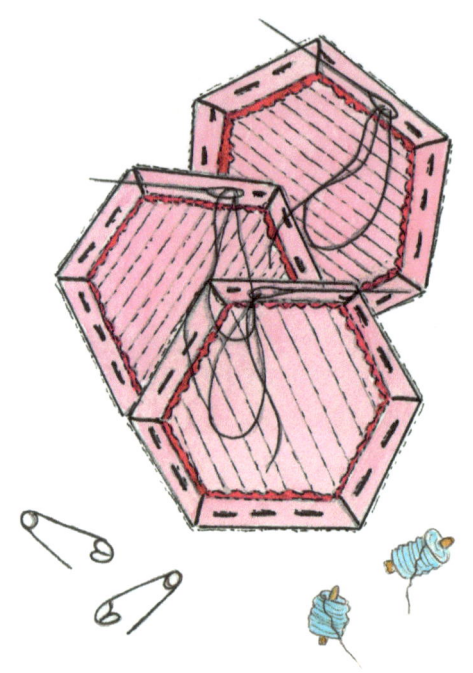

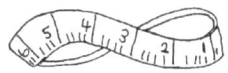

"Do you still have some of that material I had last week? Only, I couldn't get back as my husband was dead in his chair when I got home, and I was worried as I couldn't find your phone number and thought you may have sold out!!!"

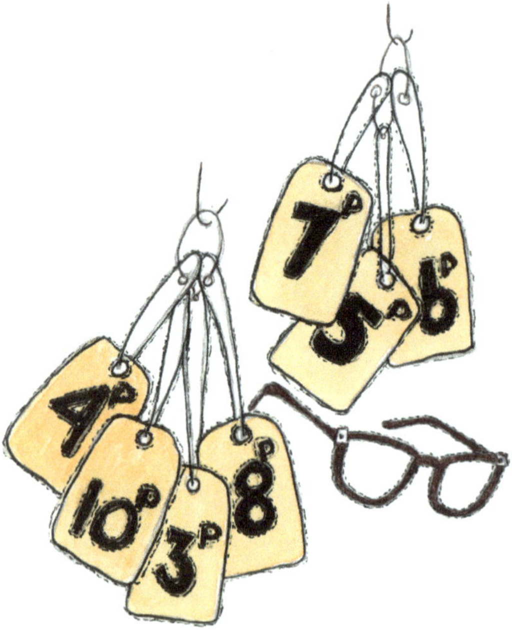
4p
10p
3p
8p
7p
5p
6p

"Could you repair my glasses?"

"No sir! We sell material!"

"Yes but it is only a small screw at the side to repair —"

"NO SIR!"

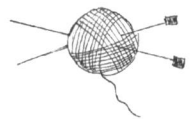

"Do you have any sweatshirt material? Only, I'm doing a survey for my daughter, and she will be wanting a FULL YARD!"

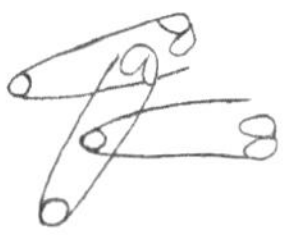

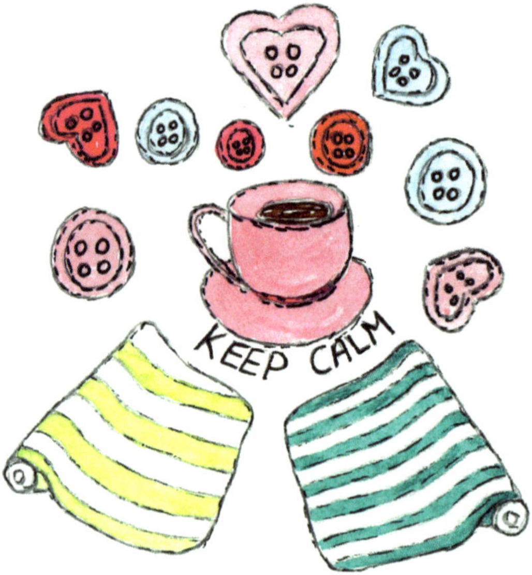
KEEP CALM

Two hippies standing outside the shop. One goes inside, looks around and shouts to her friend outside...

"No don't come in, there is only stuff in here other people don't want!!"

"I really like this material very much. If I buy some now, can you guarantee I will be able to buy some more in 2 years?"

"Do you have any scraps of fabric that you are throwing out? As I would like to make A JACKET!"

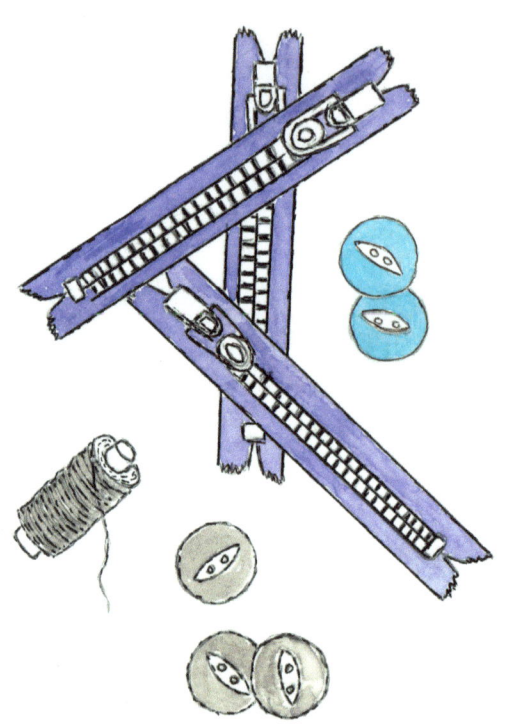

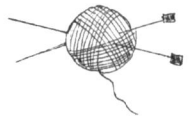

"Do you have a zip, please?"

"Yes, what length do you want?"

"Oh! I thought that they were all the same length!"

CENTRE BACK
ZIP
BACK CUT 2
FRONT

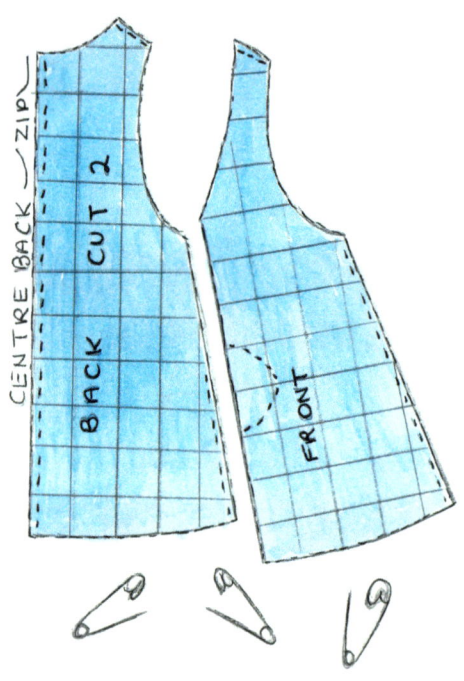

"Do you sell fabric as well as material?"

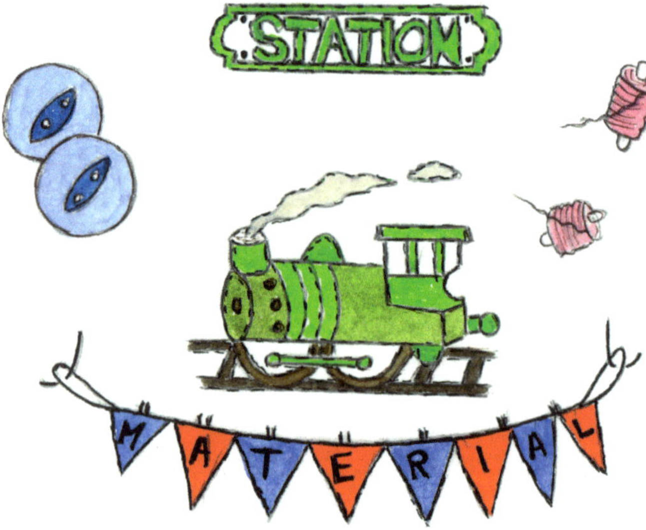
STATION
MATERIAL

"Do you know the train times to Falmouth?"

"We are a fabric shop!!!"

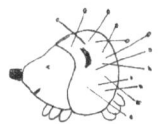

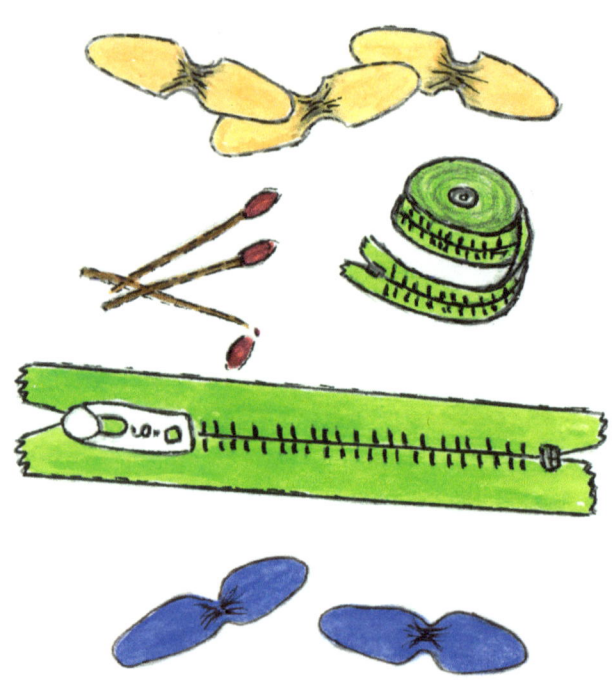

"Do you sell matches without the red blobs on the end?"

"Do you sell woggles? (i.e. toggles)"

"Do you sell zips on a roll?"

S·D TEXTILES
PRETTY FUNNY!

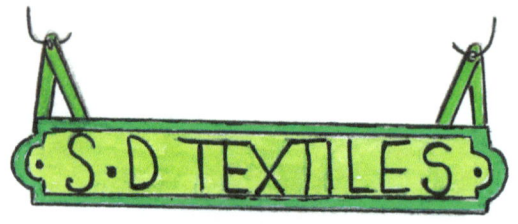

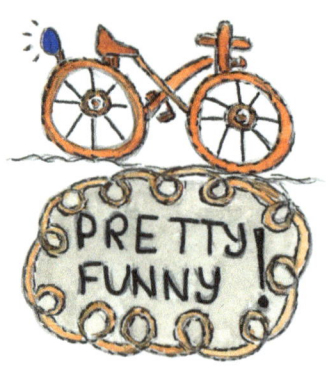

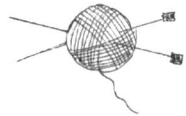

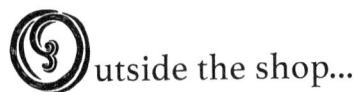utside the shop...

"Oi mate, are you going to be standing out here for a while? If so, could you watch my bike while I go inside the shop two doors down?"

Answer: "NO!!!"

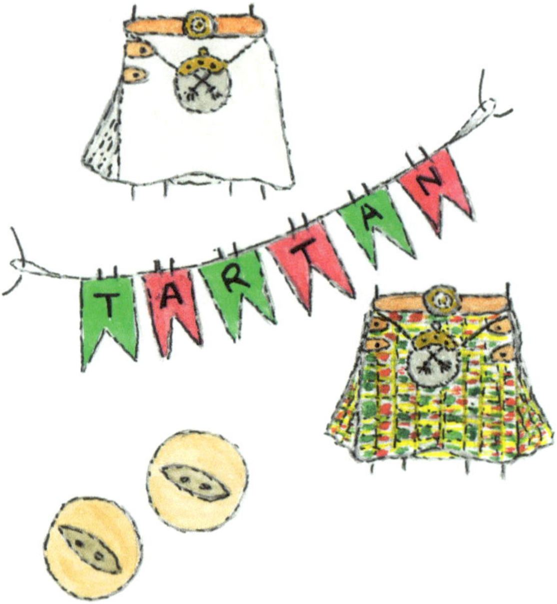
TARTAN

"Do you have tartan material?"

"YES!"

"No do you have a plain one?"

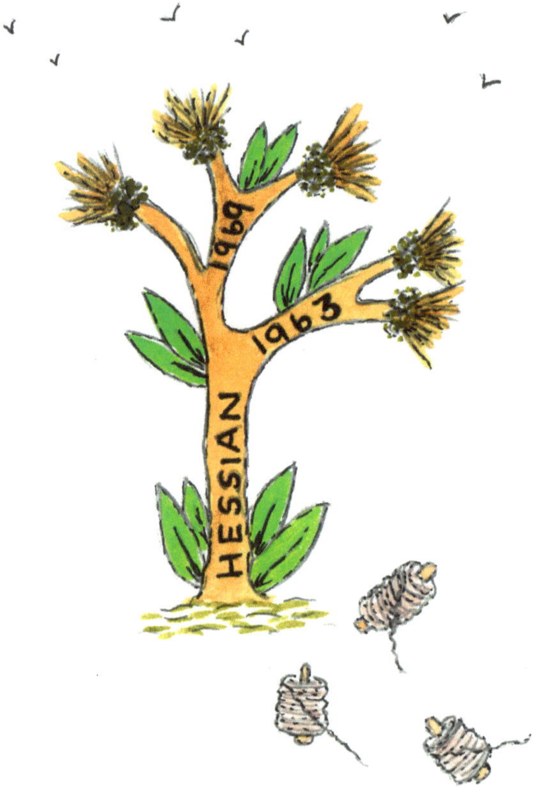
1969
1963
HESSIAN

"Can you tell me what tree that hessian comes from and what year it was picked?"

"Could I have a portion of elastic?"

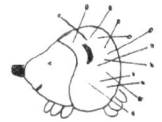

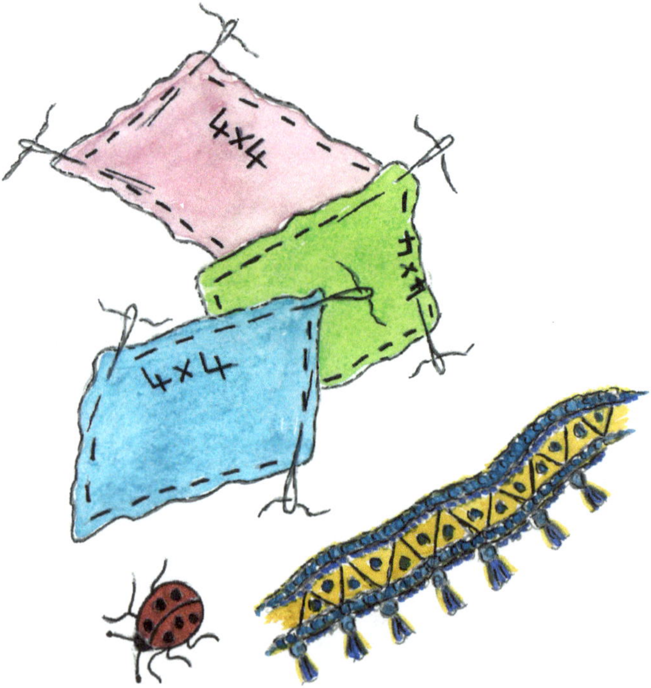
4x4
4x4
4x4

"Does the material come already stitched up? I only need 4x4!"

"Do you sell Celtic knotwork braid, cheap?"

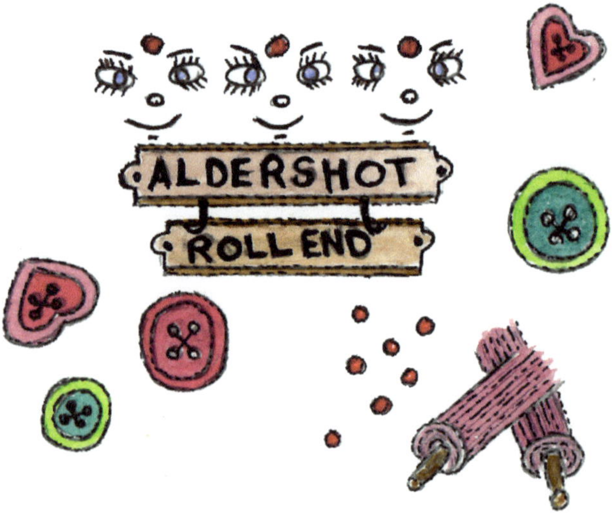
ALDERSHOT
ROLL END

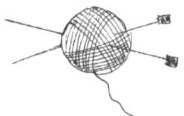

"Do you sell spots for the middle of your forehear like Indians wear?"

"My mother does handy crafts, is there anywhere that she can buy 'ends of rolls' in ALDERSHOT!?!"

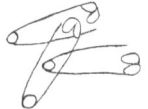

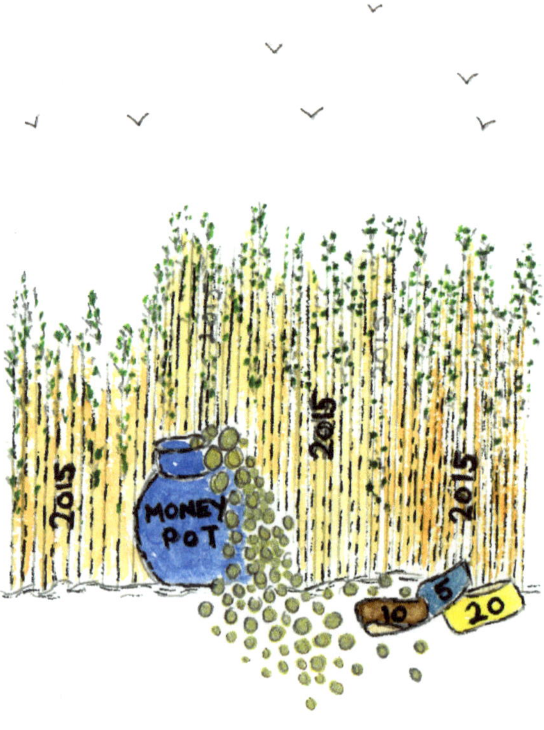
2015
MONEY POT
2015
2015
10
5
20

"This natural linen, could you tell me if it is from this year's, or last year's crop? Only, I can't buy it yet, as I haven't got any money."

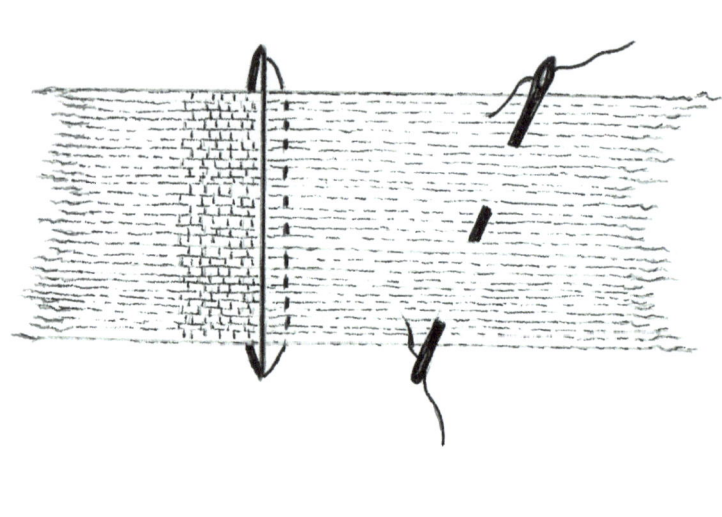

£1 a yard calico...

"Could you tell me if it is hand-woven?"

"Do you sell deep-sea natural sponges?"

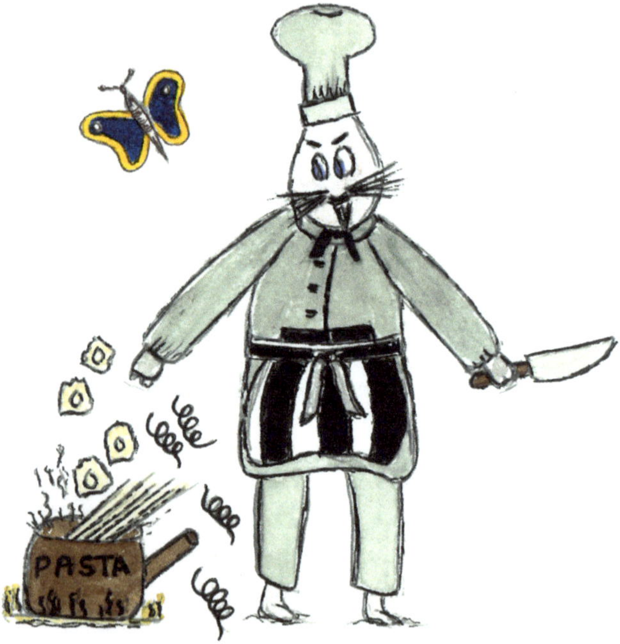
PASTA

Lady waiting to be served outside the shop...

"Can I help you, Madam?"

Her reply – "Pasta!"

"Sorry, what did you say?"

"Pasta!"

"What about it?"

"Do you have any?"

"Madam this is a fabric shop!"

Her reply – "Well do you have any anyway?"

"No, please leave!"

Reply – "What an attitude, you don't have to be so nasty!!!"

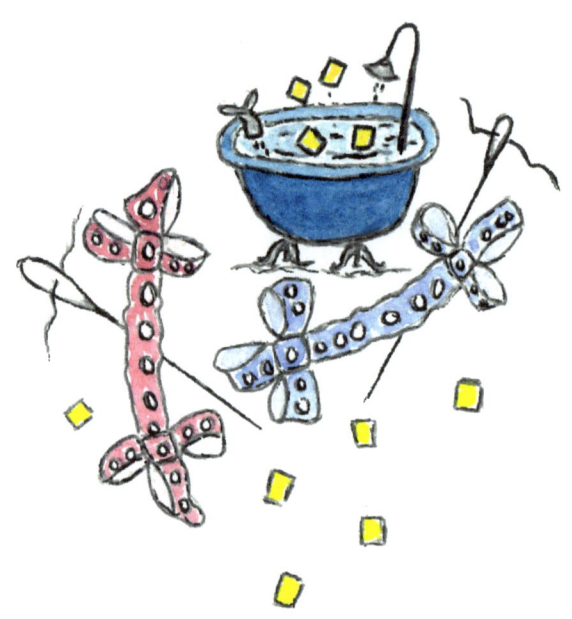

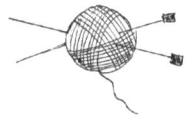

A lady in the shop opens a paper bag with small bath cubes inside.

She says, "Do you want to swap these bath cubes for some ribbon?"

"No Madam."

"Well, if I bring some needles in next week, will you swap them for ribbon?"

"No"

"Oh, so you don't swap here?"

"NO!"

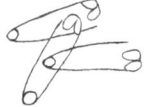

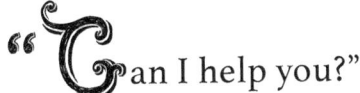

"No thanks, I am looking for something I have never seen before!"

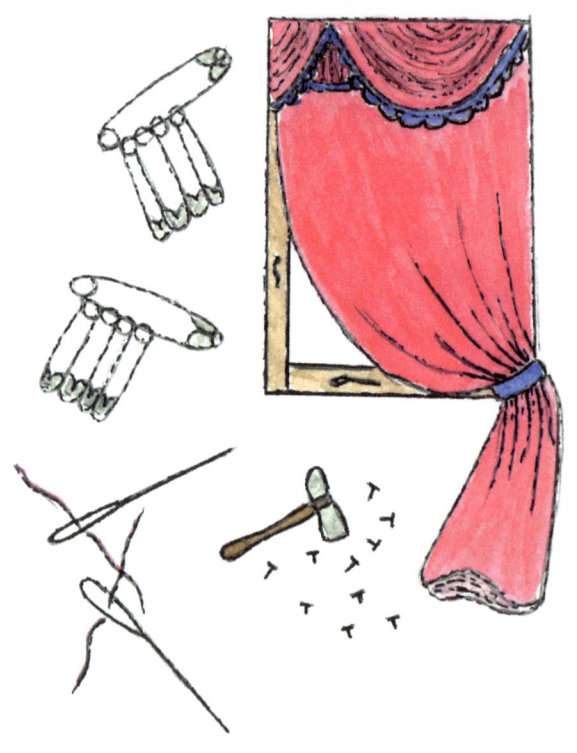

"I would like some curtains in my lounge, and I like that fabric over there. How do you get them up there? Or will you put them up for me?"

"Do you sell off-cuts of wallpaper?"

"Do you sell straw by the yard?"

"Do you sell handmade shirts?"

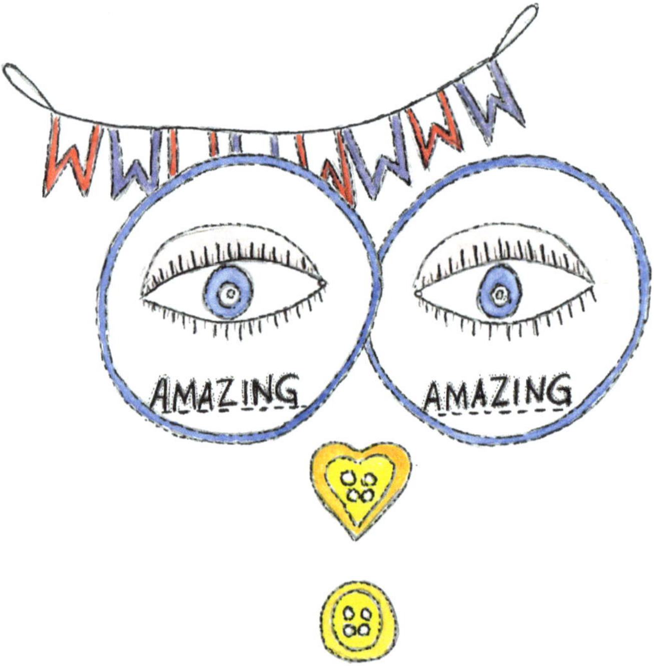
AMAZING
AMAZING

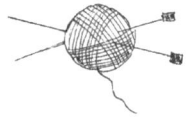

A lady came up to me and pointed to David and said, "Is he still here?"

I said, "No" and laughed, and so did David.

She said, "But you used to be here, didn't you?"

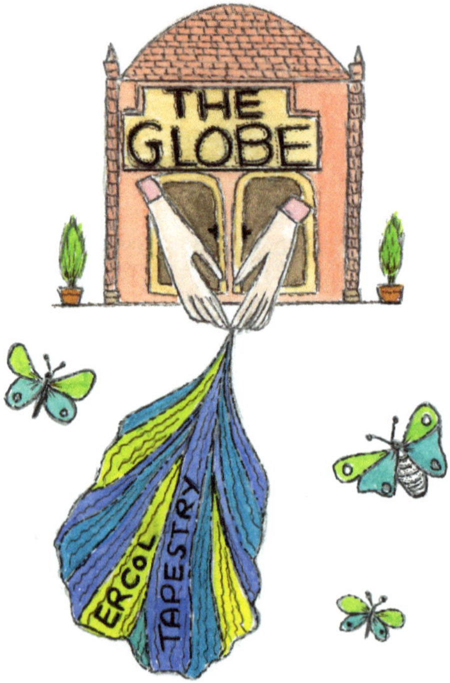
THE GLOBE
ERCOL
TAPESTRY

"I am looking for material 30-40 years old, used by Ercol furniture. It is a medieval tapestry design of two people holding hands with The Globe Theatre in the background. It's very rare!

"I thought you might pull out ½ a yard, dusty and dirty and say... There you are, just the piece you need!"

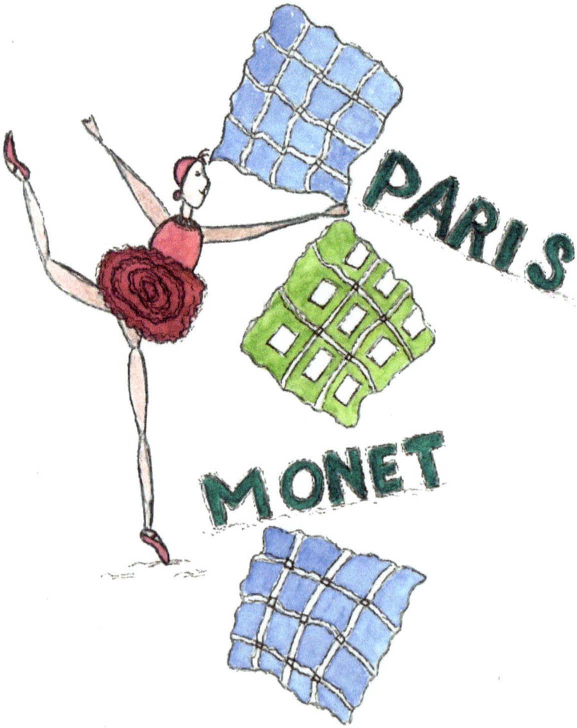
PARIS
MONET

"Do you have any muslin with squares and lines on?"

Answer: "No"

"...only, I have seen some in the Monet House in Paris and that's what I want".

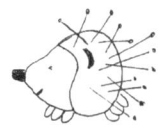

"How much is that whole roll of fabric? Thank you and don't forget to put something on for yourself!"

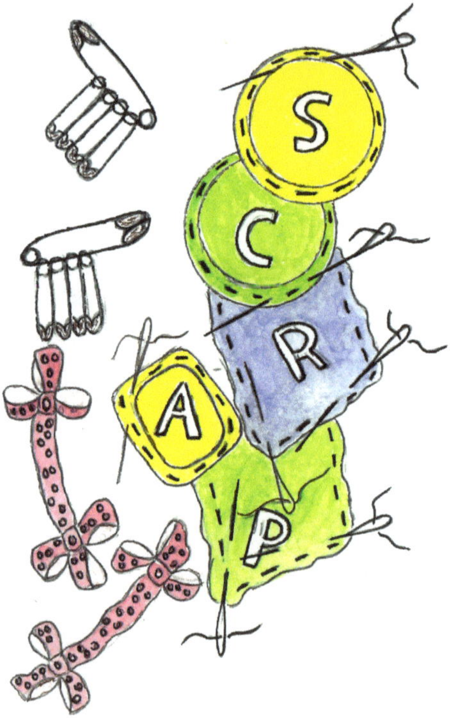
S
C
R
A
P

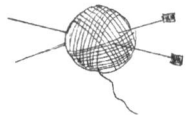

"Do you have any shreds of fabric?"

"Do you have a selection of scraps?"

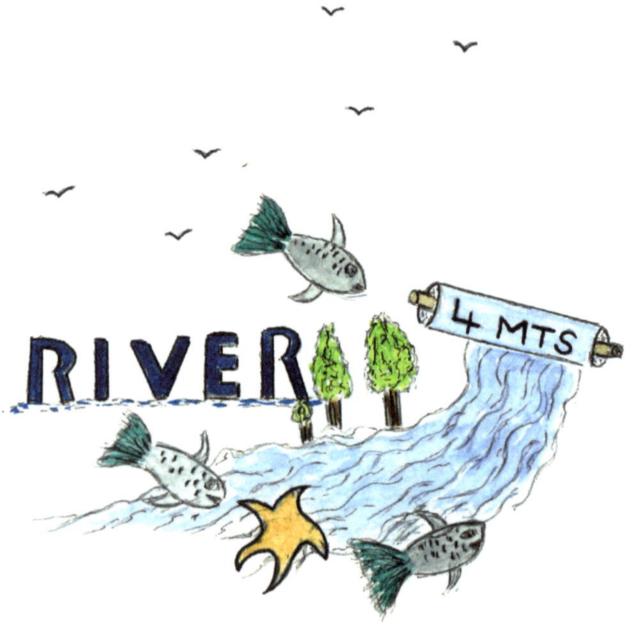
RIVER
4 MTS

"Do you have any offcuts of blue fabric?"

"Yes, how big do you need it?"

"About 4 metres long."

"Do you like this piece of blue fabric?"

"Oh no, it must be the colour of the Limpopo River!"

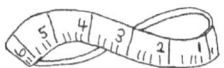

"**W**e are starting our own business, could you supply us with rolls of fabric, and can we pay it off at £2 a week?"

GREY
Gray
THAT GREY

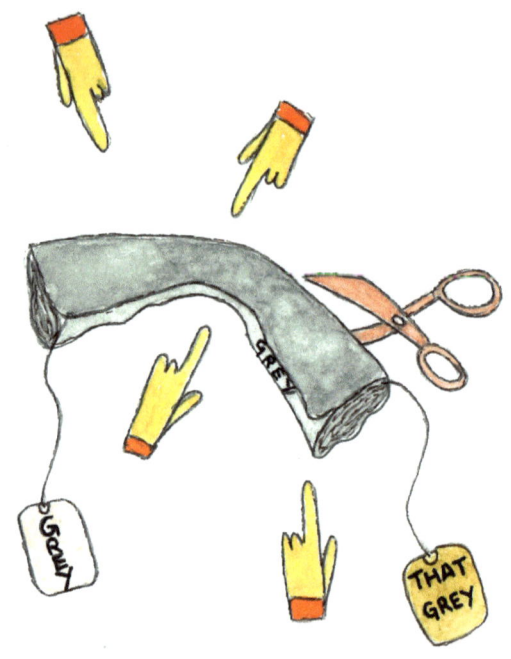

"Do you have THAT grey material?"

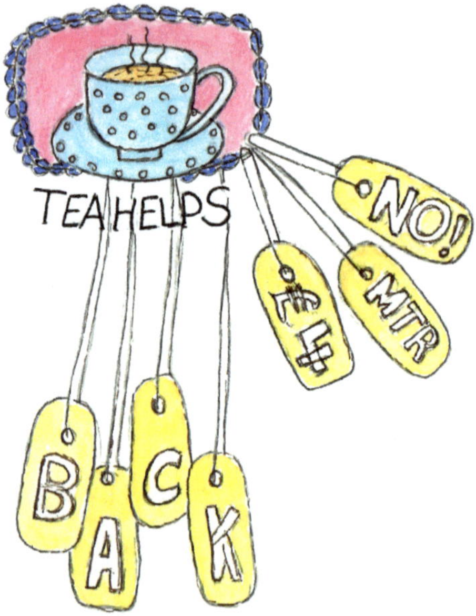
TEA HELPS
B
A
C
K
£4
MTR
NO!

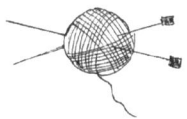

"Could I have a metre of that fabric? I will only be using it once, so will you buy it back when I have used it?"

"NO!"

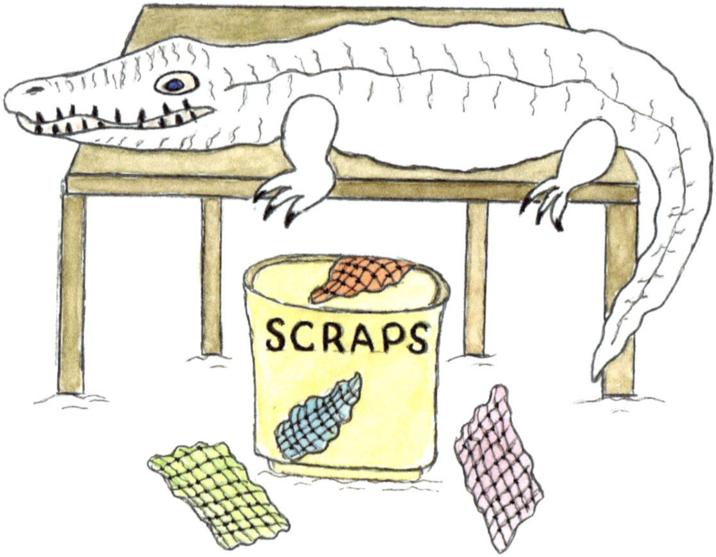
SCRAPS

"Do you have any very deep and thick crocodile skin in white?"

"Do you have one-off scraps large enough to cover my table?"

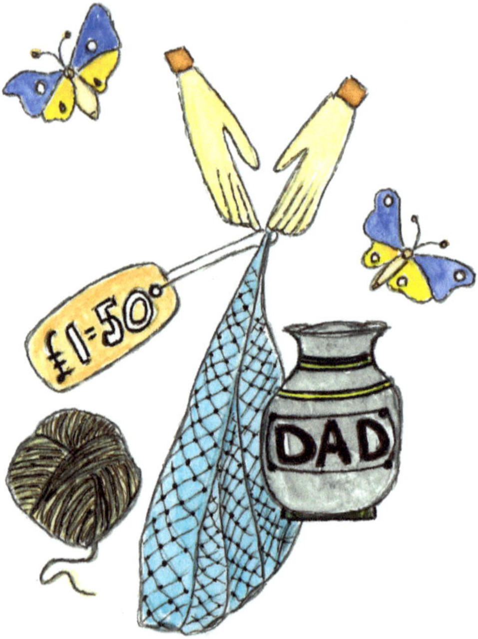
£1-50
DAD

"I like that fabric at £1.50 a metre but will think about it while on my way back from picking up my husband's ashes!"

"Do you have any scraps of string?"

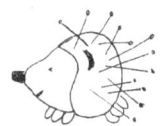

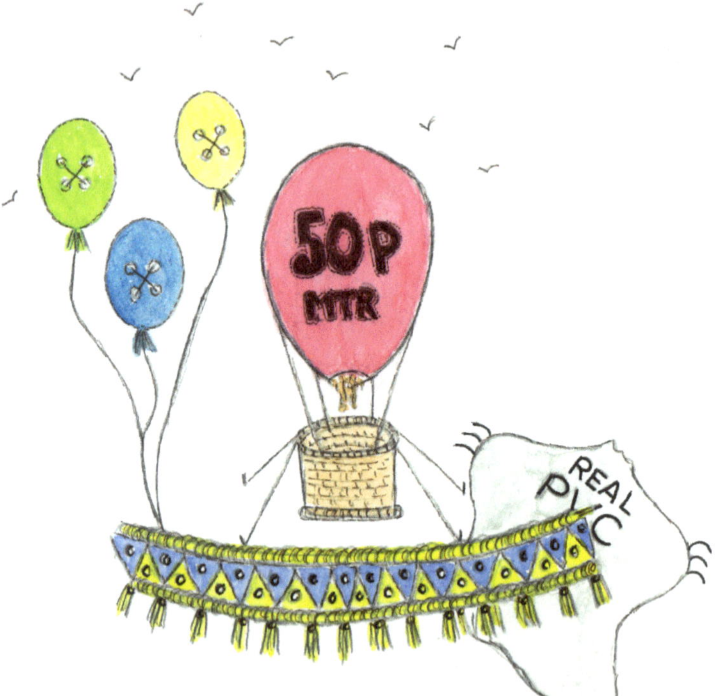
50P
MTR
REAL
PVC

"Do you have any material for making hot air balloons?"

"Do you sell Edelweiss braids?"

"Is that PVC plastic 60" wide real leather?"

"NO!"

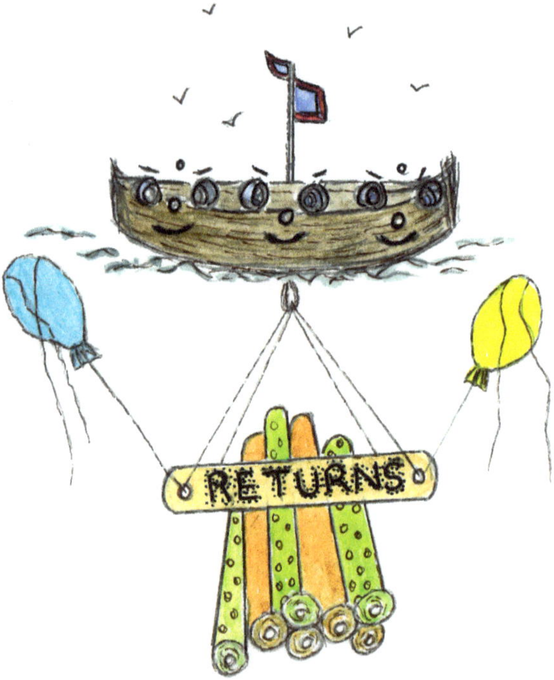
RETURNS

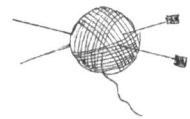

"Do you hire out materials for parties and events?"

"Can I help you, sir?"

"No thanks, I am just floating!"

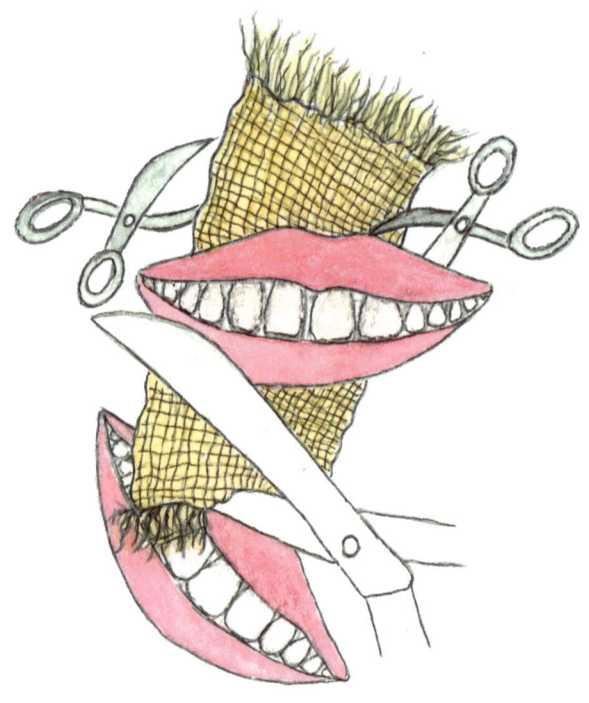

"I would like 2 metres of hessian fabric, please. How are you going to cut it?"

Answer: "I am using scissors these days as my teeth are blunt!!!"

(no reaction at all)

The jewellery shop 3 doors down...

"Do you have a cross with a BLOKE ON IT?"

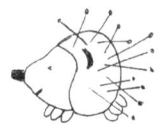

Electric shop 5 doors down...

"Could you shorten this cord on my electric kettle, as I would like it to BOIL QUICKER?"

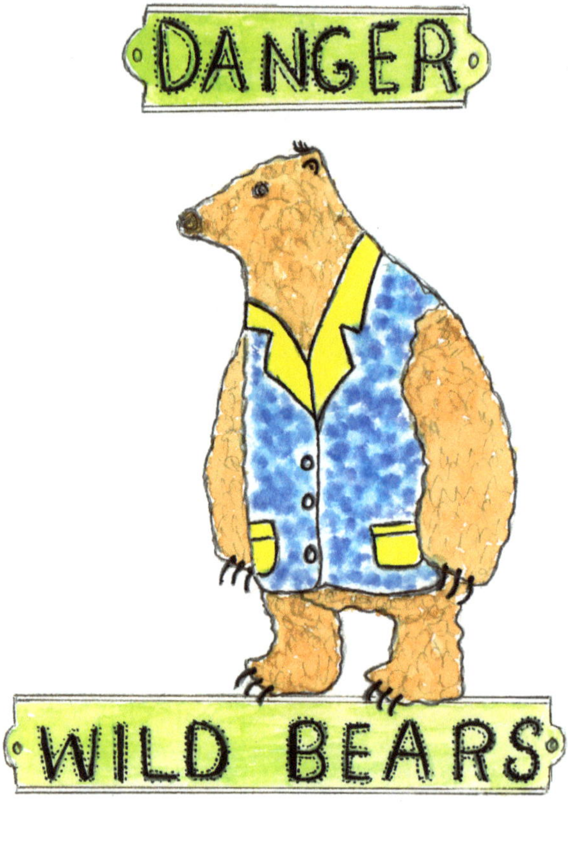
DANGER
WILD BEARS

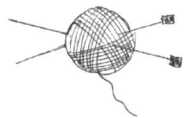

"What do you have to make a coat?"

"We have this very nice fur fabric at 60" wide."

"Oh no sorry, I cannot wear anything that comes from an animal!!!"

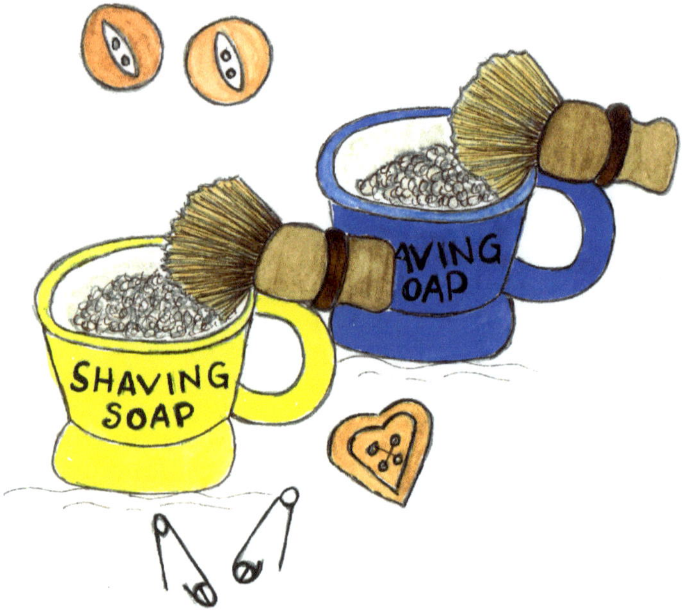
SHAVING
SOAP
AVING
OAP

"Can I have a shaving soap, please?"

"We sell material sir!"

"...but I always get it here!"

"No, you can't have!"

"Oh yes, I do...every single week!"

"Hi, do you have a selection of casserole dishes?"

_____

"Do you sell inch squares of fabric?"

_____

"Do you have a box with free materials in it?"

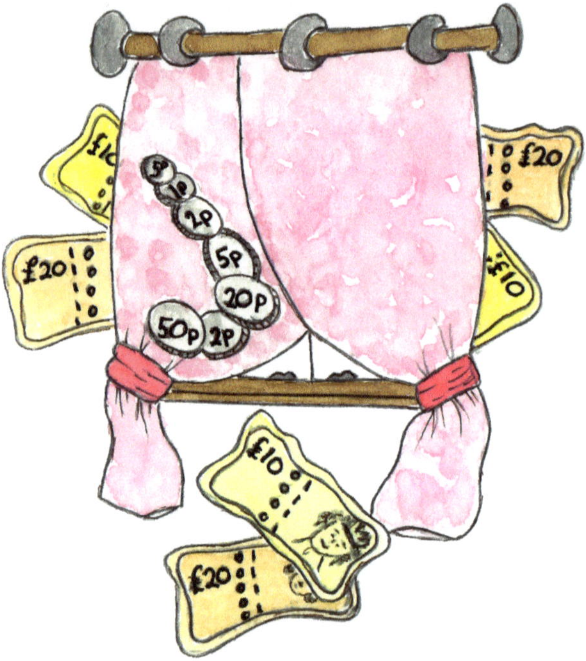
£20
£20
£10
2p
5p
20p
50p
2p
£10
£20

"Do you have any cheap pink material for a very small kitchen window?"

"Yes, I have this one at £1.50 a yard."

"Oh no thanks, I didn't want it to cost me a fortune."

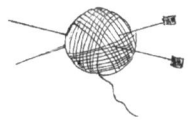

Outside the shop...

"Do you have fasteners for bras?"

"No, I am sorry."

"Okay, so do you have any inside the shop then?"

"Do you have moulds for making your own buckles?"

"Any olive-green marabou?"

"Have you got a 19-yard remnant of 72" wide cotton print?"

"Do you sell rubberised horsehair?"

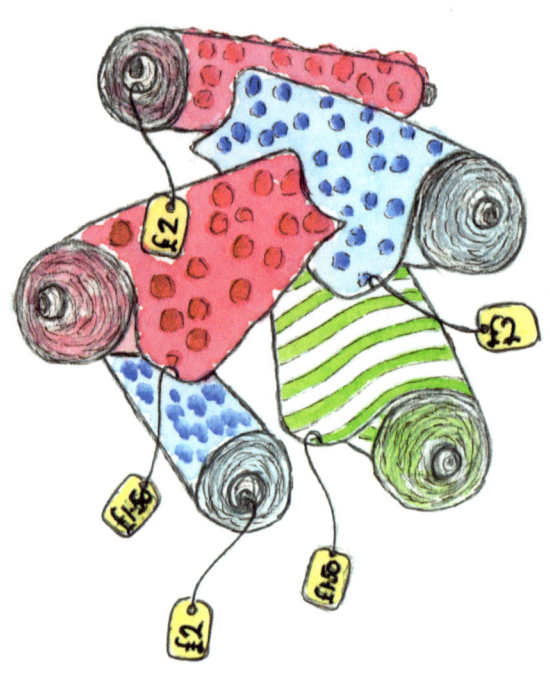

"**D**o you give a discount for bulk buying, because I need 3 yards?"

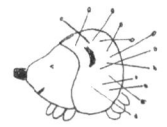

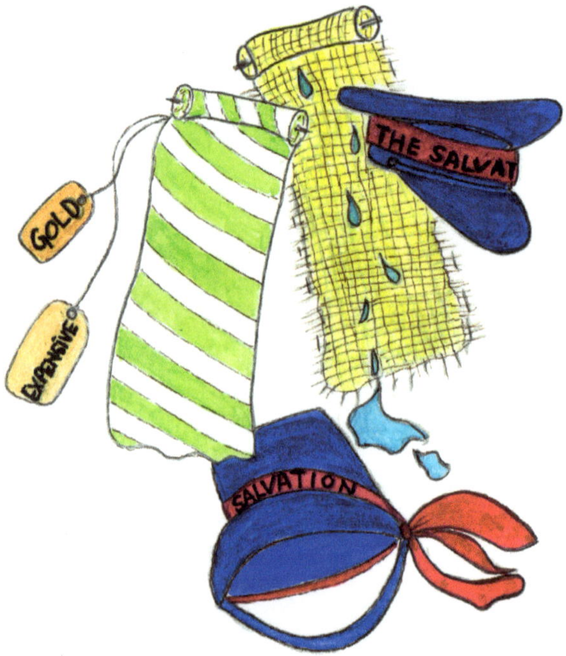
GOLD
EXPENSIVE
THE SALVAT
SALVATION

"Do you have any curtain lining?"

"Yes, this is £1.49 a yard."

"I'm not looking for anything MEGGA expensive like that!"

"Is that net waterproof?"

"Do you sell Salvation Army hats?"

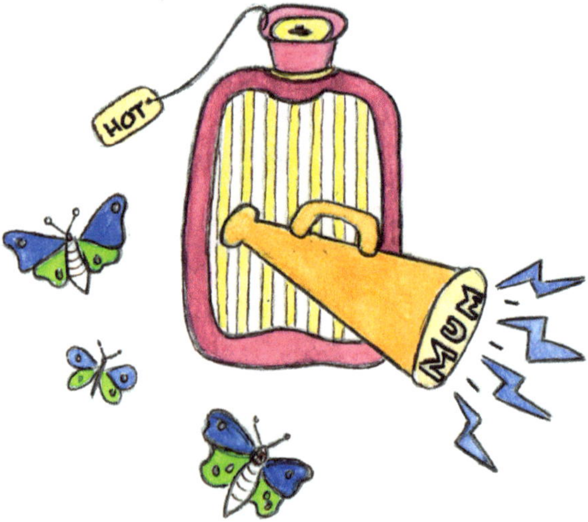
HOT
MUM

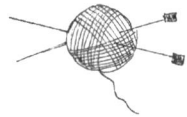

 lady shouting from inside the shop to outside…

"No…he ain't not got none, mum!!!"

"Do you sell hot water bottles?"

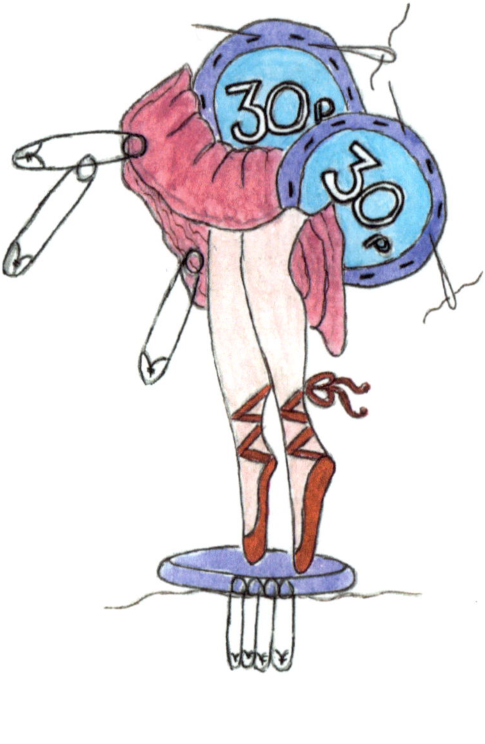
30p
30p

"Do you have any safety pins?"

"Yes, we have a bunch for 30p."

"Oh, I only wanted one and it will be such a waste buying too many. I will leave it; I will ask my sister for one as I know she has one!"

CK
CK
CK

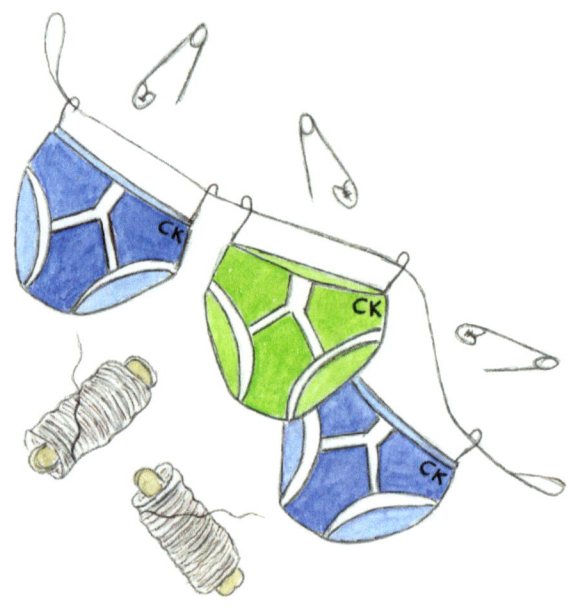

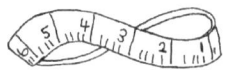

"Do you have some elastic? It is only for my father's pants who is 90 years old and I don't want to spend too much as he is going to die soon!

"Well you have to be practical DON'T YOU!!"

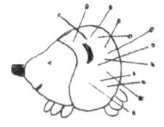

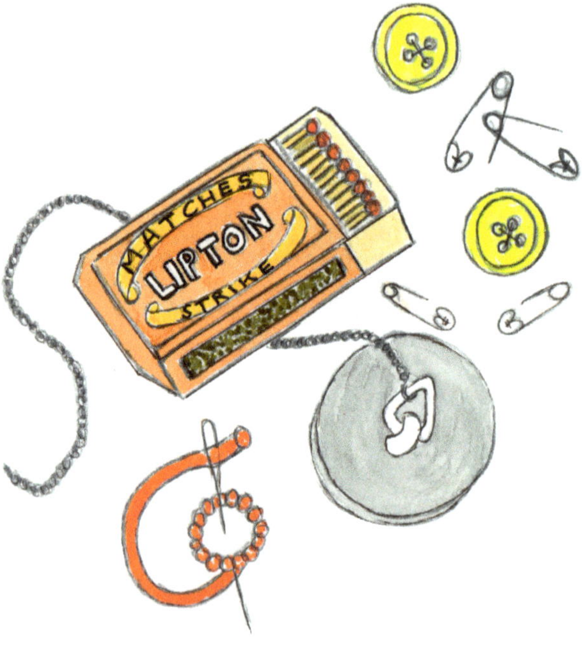
MATCHES
LIPTON
STRIKE

"Can I have a box of matches, please?"

"We are a fabric shop, Madam!"

"Can I have a bath plug then, please?"

"We sell fabric - NO!"

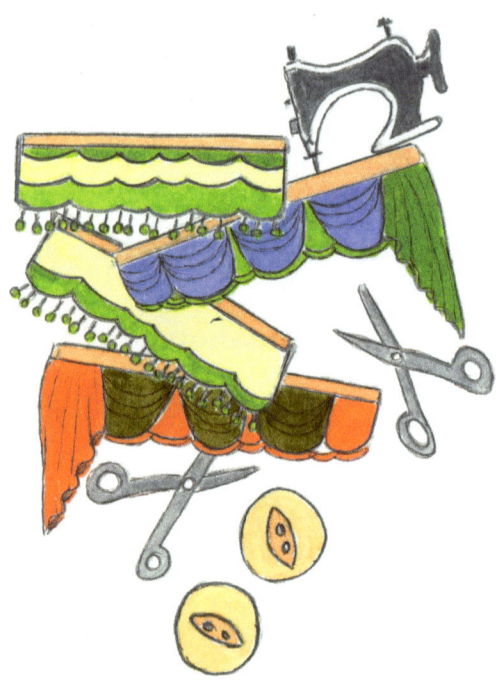

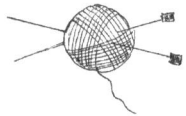

 lady came in with a shaped pelmet and asked, "Do you have some fringe to replace this?"

"Yes, here is the exact match!"

"Oh no, it has to be this curved type?"

"Do you have 'DRAKTELLA' curtain lining?"

"What???"

"Do you sell button-covering machines?"

"Do you sell toilet paper?"

"NO, we sell fabric, by the roll!"

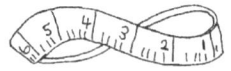

"Do you have a 6-yard oddment of stair carpet?"

"No sir!"

"Only, it's to cover four steps and a landing."

"No sir!"

"Okay thanks, I will be back when I have more time. Thank you so much."

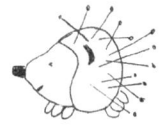

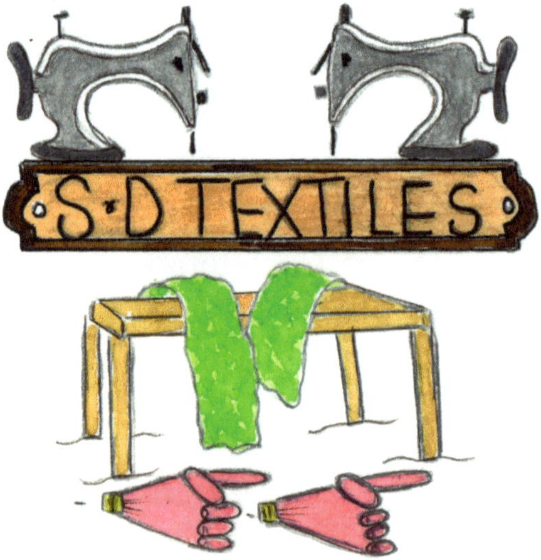
S·D TEXTILES

We displayed plain green and plain red fabric on the table outside the shop.

A lady said, "Do you have these 2 colours inside the shop?"

Answer: "WHAT!?!"

"Do you have OLD catalogues for sewing machines?"

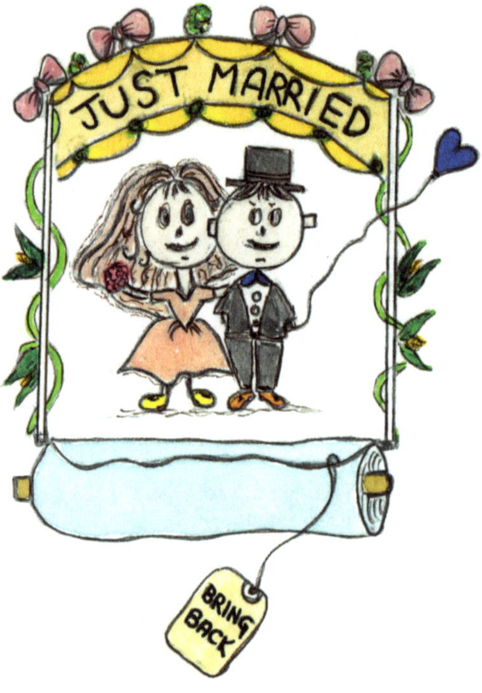
JUST MARRIED
BRING BACK

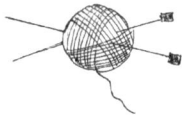

"I am getting married and don't want it to cost too much money, so can I hire the material from you and then bring it back after the wedding?"

Answer: NO!

"Could I have some of that heavy calico canvas to cover a sofa and when I get paid for covering it, can I bring the money in to pay for it?"

"Are you joking?"

Customer: "NO!"

"If I leave my shoes with you (the ones he was wearing!), could you personalise them for me with pieces of leather and fur fabric?"

"No!"

"Okay, I will have a small piece of tiger fur fabric then".

As he was paying, he said;
"Do you make lots of money here?"

"Oh yes, I have a mansion in the Bahamas! Wow, you ask some wakey questions and I am writing a book with questions just like yours in it."

He said, "Am I going in it?"

"OH YES!!!"

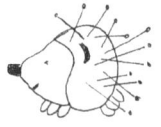

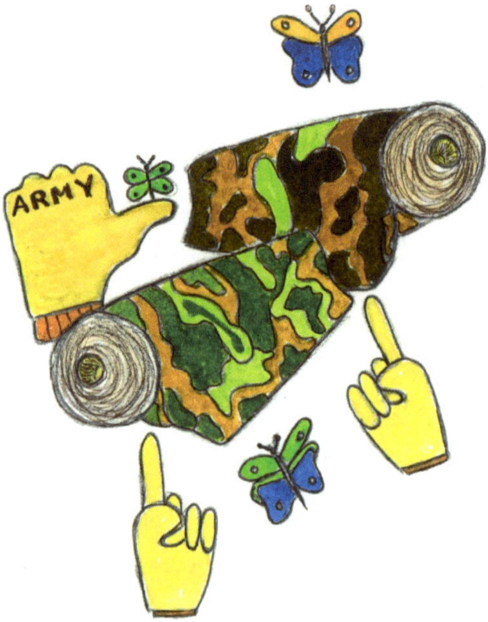
ARMY

A man is looking at the camouflage fleece...

"Sorry mate, it would be no good for me as it is too SICKY".

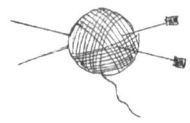

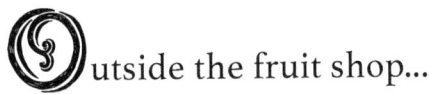

Outside the fruit shop...

A woman is trying to get coins into a jammed parking meter. Thumping the meter, she shouted into the greengrocer located opposite, "I say, your parking meter is not working."

"I am a fruit shop Madam; I don't own those meters!"

"Oh, I suppose you would be interested if I picked up my skirt and showed you my knickers"

"Maybe if you were 30 years younger my dear!"

1.8 MTS
BACK
CENTRE BACK
ZIP
FRONT

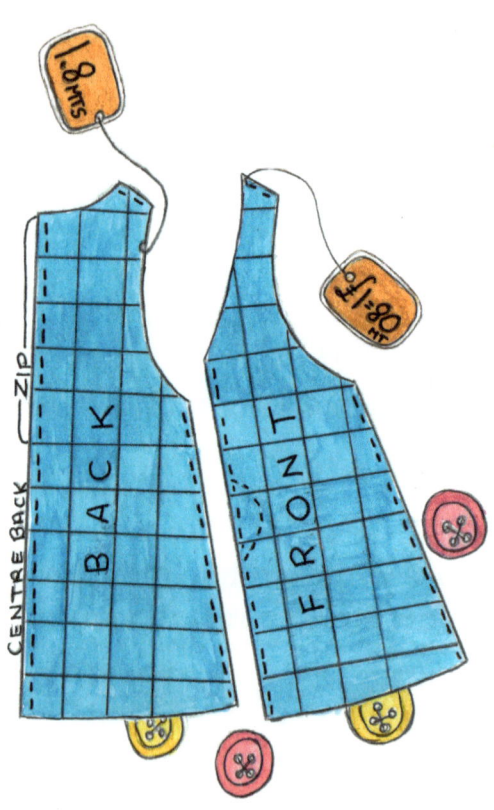

A customer came into the shop with a Vogue pattern of a ball gown and asked:

"Do you have this fabric, please?"

"No madam, that is extremely expensive fabric".

"Oh no it isn't, it says here that it is £1.80 per metre".

"No! It says you need 1.8 metres!"

She left the shop not convinced.

"Do you have a TUNISIAN crochet hook?"

"Have you got any material for a pair of SHALLOTS, as they do stop your legs from rubbing together at the top!"

"Do you mean 'CULOTTES'?"

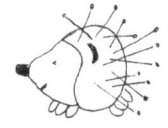

3 for £10
£9.99
£9.99

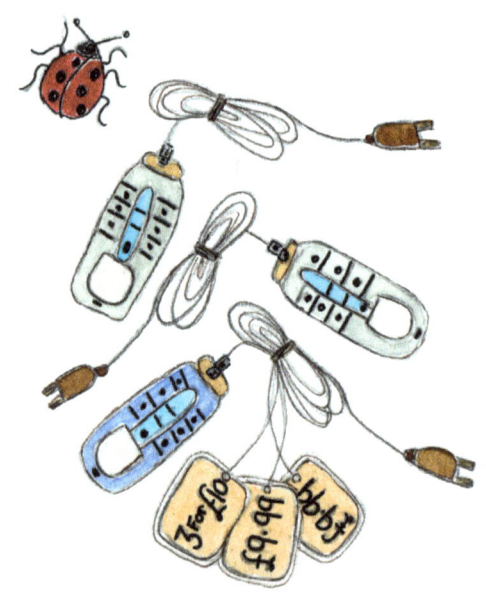

Jim's stall down the road

"How much are those phone chargers?"

Answer: "£9.99 each."

"Could you do me 3 for £10?"

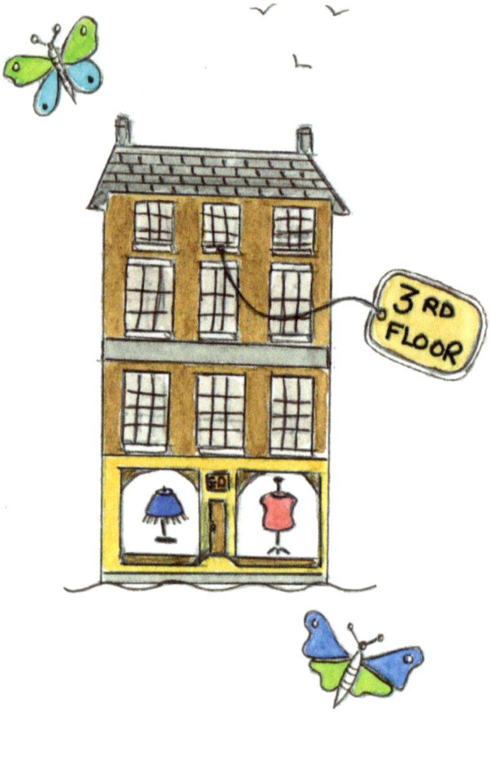
3 RD
FLOOR

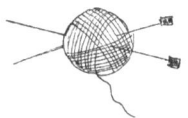

𝓕urniture Department Store window
poster a few doors down...

Bargain Basement on the
THIRD FLOOR

S·D TEXTILES
25p

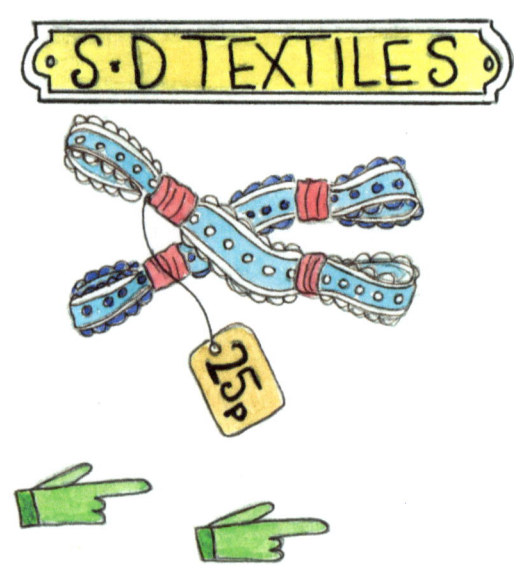

"I would like this bundle of lace at 25p, please. Do you have any other blue lace I can see?"

"Yes, there is this one at 60p a yard".

"How much would I get of that then?"

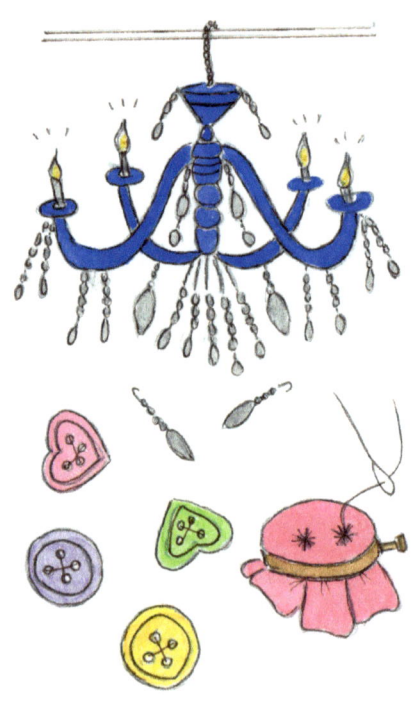

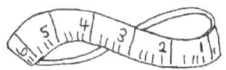

"Do you have any chandelier drops?"

"No Madam, you are in a fabric shop."

"...but I only need two like this!"

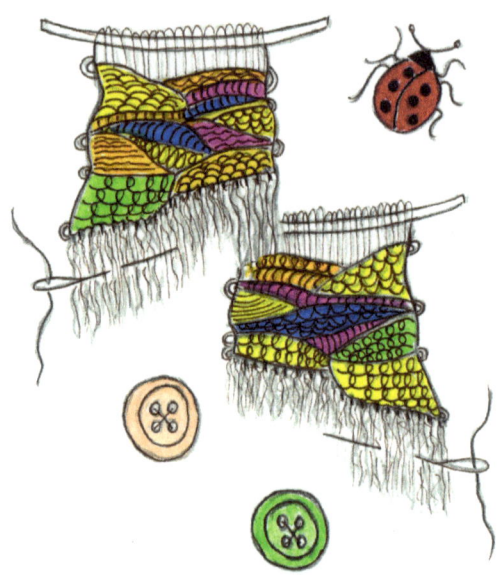

"Do you sell PERSIAN TAPESTRY material cheap!!!?"

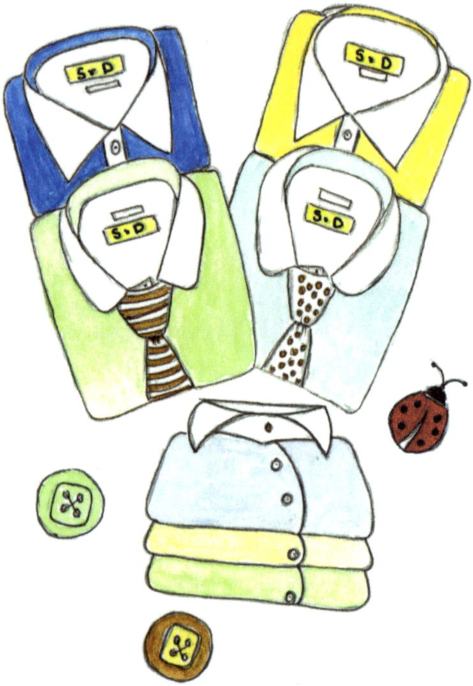
S·D
S·D
S·D
S·D

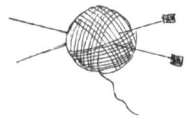

"Do you sell handmade shirts...

CHEAP?"

"Do you sell wallpaper or anything to do with it? Or scraps of wallpaper?"

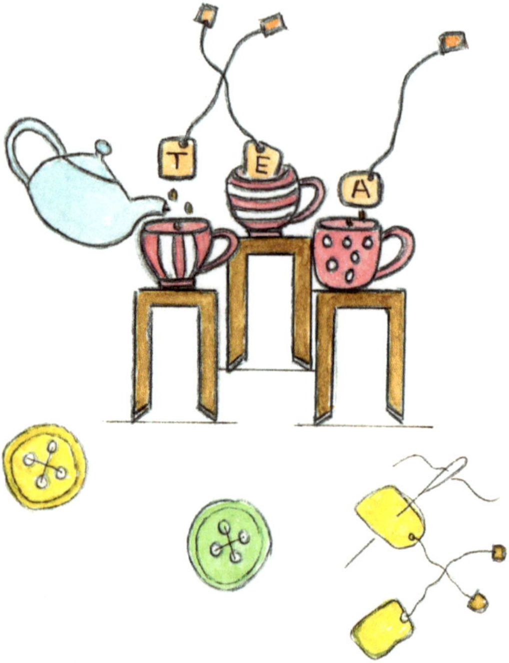
T
E
A

"Do you sell empty TEA BAGS?"

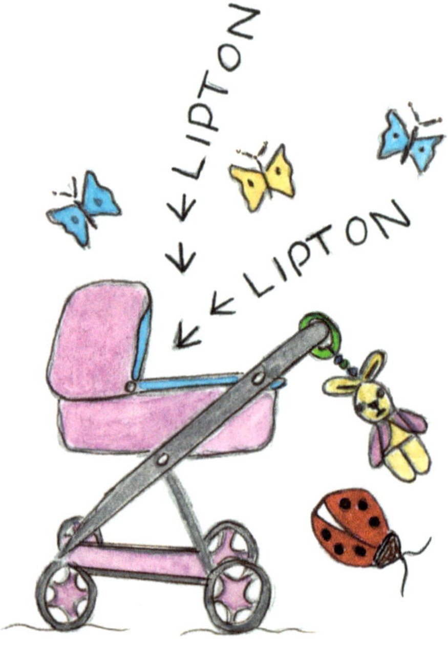
LIPTON
LIPTON

 mother shouts to her child in a pram right outside the shop...

Shut up LIPTON you misery!!

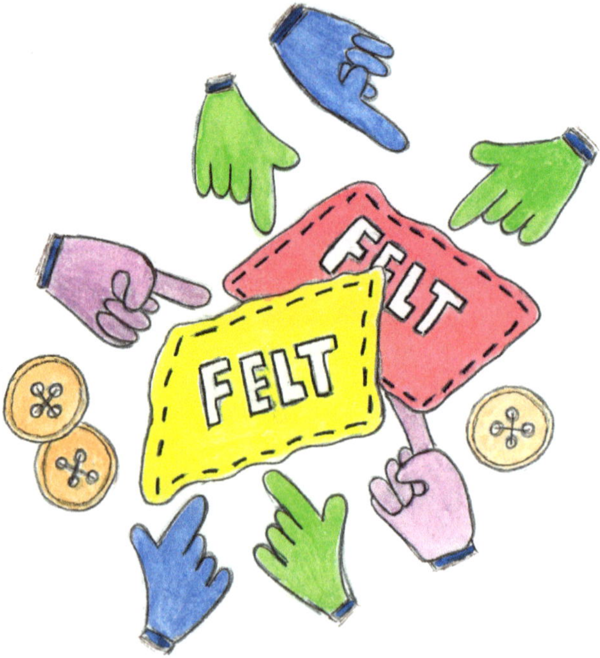
FELT
FELT

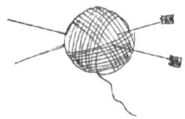

"**Is** this the place I can get felt?"

"No madam, we do that service in the back of the shop!"

No reaction!

She then proceeded to the back of the shop.

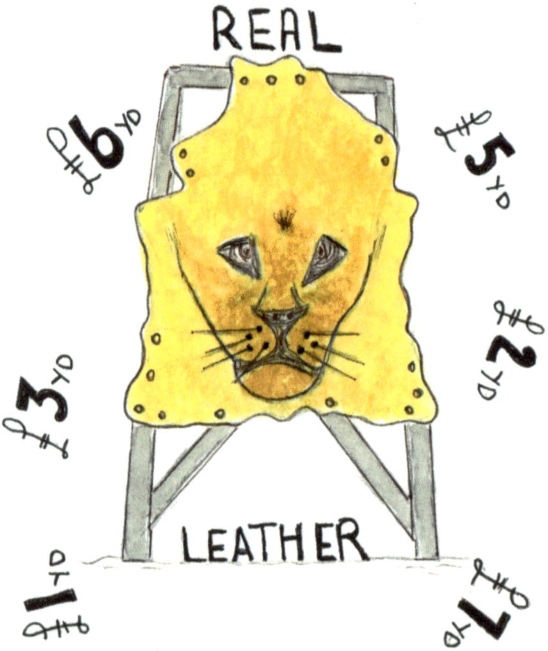
REAL
£6YD
£5YD
£3YD
£2YD
LEATHER
£1YD
£7YD

"Do you sell real leather by the yard?"

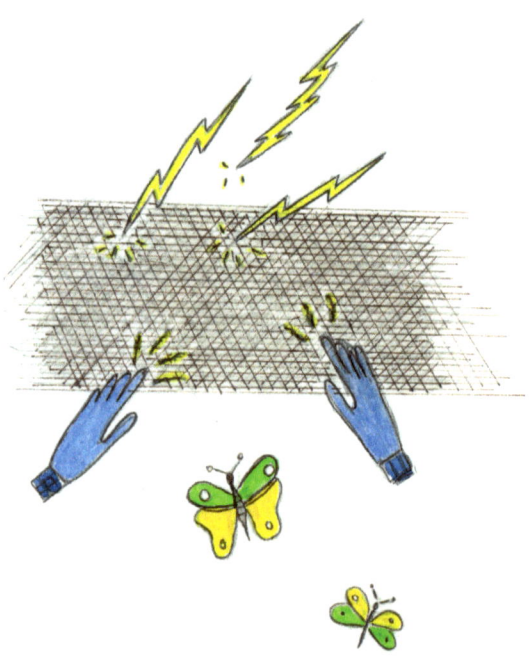

"Do you have material that conducts electricity?"

"Oh okay, what about wire mesh then?"

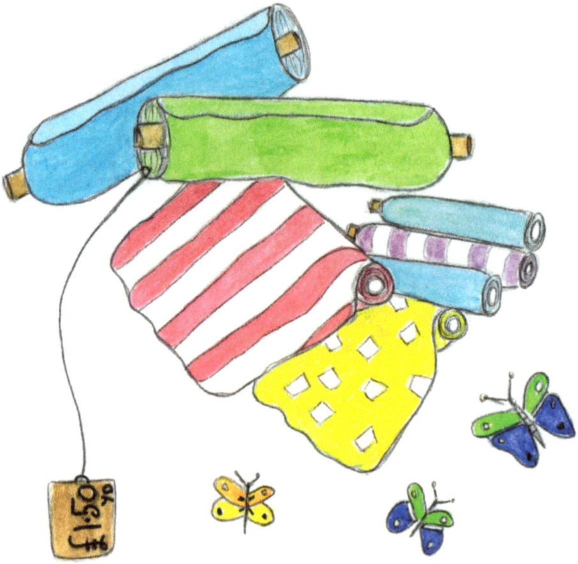
£1.50 YD

"How much is that material?"

"£1.50 a yard."

"So how much would two yards be then?"

www.ingramcontent.com/pod-product-compliance
Lightning Source LLC
Chambersburg PA
CBHW042232090526
44587CB00006B/150